slurp

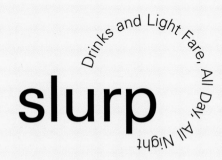

Drinks and Light Fare, All Day, All Night

nina dreyer hensley

jim hensley

paul løwe

Andrews McMeel
Publishing, LLC

Kansas City

08 09 10 11 12 WKT 10 9 8 7 6 5 4 3 2 1

ISBN-13: 978-0-7407-6990-0
ISBN-10: 0-7407-6990-1

Hensley, Nina Dreyer.
    Slurp: drinks and light fare, all day, all night / Nina Dreyer Hensley, Jim Hensley, and Paul Lowe.
        p. cm.
    ISBN-13: 978-0-7407-6990-0
    ISBN-10: 0-7407-6990-1
    1. Beverages. 2. Cocktails 3. Cookery I. Hensley, Jim. Lowe, Paul III. Title.
    TX815.H46 2008
    641.2—dc22
                            2007035698

Cover: Lise Mosveen and Pernille Ville Våge
Design: Lise Mosveen and Pernille Ville Våge

First published in 2005 by Gyldendal Norsk Fortlag, P.O. Box 6860, St. Olavs Plass, 0130 Oslo, Norway

Thanks to PR POLHEM, Kristin Van Hersch, and Gunnar Strømsholm

The following contributed props for the book: Sagaform, R.O.O.M., Habitat, Heals, Designers Guild, Conran Shop, Martha by Mail, Pier One

www.andrewsmcmeel.com

drink accessories

2

morning

17

daytime

55

evening

105

cecubeslimeshotscr
shedicefunthingsfort
edrinksicecubeslimes
hotscrushedicefunthi
ngsforthedrinksicecub
eslimeshotscrushedi
efunthingsforthedrink
sicecubeslimeshotscr
ushedicefunthingsfo
hedrinksicecubeslim

drink accessories

tasty ice cubes

Berries and herbs can be frozen inside ice cubes.
Fill an ice tray with, for example, blueberries,
raspberries, mint, or salvia. Top up with water
and freeze.

Ten good reasons to have a cocktail party

1. An anniversary.

2. You quit smoking six months ago.

3. Inauguration of a new kitchen.

4. It's Wednesday!

5. New episodes of *Ugly Betty*.

6. It's Gandhi's birthday (October 2).

7. First day of winter.

8. You got a pay raise.

9. It's a full moon.

10. You really have nothing else to do!

Ice cubes can be used for so much more than keeping a drink cold. They can also provide additional flavor and color. All juices can be frozen; for example, orange, cranberry, and pineapple juice.

You can also make ice cubes filled with orange, lemon or lime zest. It gives the drinks a sour twist.

4

Ten great tips for a perfect party

1. Enough drinks—it is better to have too many than too few.

2. Funny people—think seriously about who you invite; make it a good mix.

3. Something to snack on—preferably more than peanuts and potato chips.

4. Dim the lights and light lots of candles.

5. Good music.

6. Enough ice.

7. Enough seating—use ottomans and floor cushions.

8. Make sure everyone has a good time, introduce people, and be a good host.

9. Tell the neighbors so the cops don't show up.

10. Do not do the dishes until the following day!

syrups

Syrups are a great way to add sweetness to a drink.

The basic recipe for simple syrup is 2 cups (½ L) of water and 1 cup (200 g) of sugar. Combine in a pan and boil for about 10 minutes, then let it cool. You can add flavor to the syrup with spices or herbs. Boil the spices/herbs together with the syrup and strain after it cools down.

Suggestions for flavorings:
2 cinnamon sticks
1 teaspoon (2 g) cardamom seeds
2 chile peppers
2 stalks of lemongrass
Zest of 1 lime
1 vanilla bean

garnishing

Some people can never have enough garnishes in their drinks, be it a funny stirrer, fruits, or tiny umbrellas. A colorful straw is also a great way of adding color.

These wooden stirrers with white and brown rock candy are perfect for stirring an Irish coffee.

citrus sticks

These sticks can be used for garnish on drinks or on cakes. Use a citrus peeler to peel thin strips from limes or lemons. Boil 2 cups (½ L) of water with 1 cup (200 g) of sugar. Let the peels simmer for 1 hour. Remove from the heat and let the peels cool slightly. While the peels are still warm, twist each around a tall, thin object, such as a chopstick. Put them on a plate and cover them completely with sugar. Allow them to dry overnight. Pull the peels from the chopsticks and, voilà, you will have a citrus stick you can use as a garnish.

sugared rims

Many drinks taste great with sugar around the rim of the glass. You can use regular sugar, colored sugar, sweetened chocolate powder, or crushed candy such as raspberry or lemon drops.

Rub a slice of lime around the rim of a glass and dip it in the sugar. Shake it gently to get rid of any excess sugar.

salted rims

A great margarita demands salt around the rim of the glass, preferably a gourmet salt. The salt can

also be flavored with a little grated lime zest. Rub a slice of lime around the rim of the glass and

dip it in the salt.

glassware and accessories

You do not need to go shopping for new glassware to make the drinks in this book, but be creative! Here is a short guide:

Martini glass This glass has a broad opening and a thin stem, giving it the elegance that a martini demands.

Cocktail glass Looks like a martini glass, but its bowl is more rounded.

Rocks glass A short, heavy glass with straight sides. It must be large so as to provide a good grip.

Shot glass A short and sturdy glass; must be small enough for a tiny drink.

Highball Tall and skinny, to keep the drink cold.

Champagne Also called a "flute." Tall, thin, and elegant with a narrow opening to retain the bubbles as long as possible.

Margarita A stemmed glass with a wide bowl perfect for rimming with salt.

shots

A cucumber can be used for more than just salads!

Cut up the cucumber into 2- to 3-inch (6 to 7 cm) pieces. Use a teaspoon or a melon baller and hollow out the top portion of each cucumber piece. Put the cucumber pieces on a plate and fill with vodka or other alcohol. Use a few cucumber strips as stirrers. After drinking the vodka, you can eat your glass . . . not bad!

what do I need?

Making a good cocktail can be compared to chemistry, but instead of mixing acids and liquids, we are mixing alcohol and juices. Invest in a **jigger**. It might be easier in the beginning to use a jigger until you learn how to make a visual measure. A good **shaker** is also handy; not only is it practical, but it can also look impressive as you are standing there shaking away. You can find drink sets that come with a **stirrer** and a **strainer**; a strainer is handy if you want to strain the drink into the glass.

An **ice crusher** might be a good investment as well. Crushed ice makes a drink look great. If you do not have an ice crusher, put the ice cubes in a towel and use a rolling pin to crush them. A **wooden pestle** is also good; it is awesome when you need to mash sugar and limes for a Mojito. The back of a spoon also works.

morning

moothiesjuicecafea
aitteatoastmueslibag
elyogurtsmoothiesju
cecaféaulaitteatoastm
eslibagelyogurtsmo
othiesjuicecaféaulai
eamorningmueslib
elyogurtsmoothiesju
caféaulaitteatoastm
slibagelyogurtsmoo

juices

tomato and chile juice

Serves 1

6 large, ripe plum tomatoes

¼ jalapeño, chopped finely

Ice cubes

1 chile pepper, for garnish

Bring water to a boil in a large saucepan. Cut

a cross in each of the tomatoes, and put

them into the boiling water for 30 seconds.

Remove them from the boiling water and

place them in ice water. Peel off the skins.

Run the tomatoes and chopped jalapeño

through a juice press. Pour the juice into a

glass filled with ice and garnish with the

chile.

orange, strawberry, and apricot juice

Serves 1

4 ripe apricots
8 strawberries
Juice of 2 large Valencia oranges
Ice cubes

Bring a medium-size saucepan of water to a boil. Add the apricots to the boiling water and blanch for 1 minute. Remove them from the water and plunge them into cold water. Peel off the skin and cut the apricots in half. Remove the pits. Put the apricots, strawberries, and orange juice into a blender and mix until smooth. Pour the juice into a glass filled with ice. You can also substitute grapefruit juice for the orange juice.

carrot and ginger juice

Serves 1

4 large carrots, peeled, plus ¼ cup (57 g)
   grated carrot, for garnish
1-inch (2 cm) piece of fresh ginger, peeled
Ice cubes

Run the whole carrots and ginger through a juice press. Pour the juice into a glass filled with ice and sprinkle the grated carrot on top.

tropical juice

Serves 1

Juice of 1 large orange
½ ripe mango
½ ripe papaya
1 tablespoon (15 ml) lime juice
Ice cubes
1 slice of lime, for garnish
Fresh mint, for garnish

Press the orange in a juice press. Peel the mango and cut into pieces. Peel the papaya. Put the orange juice, mango, papaya, and lime juice into a blender and blend until smooth. Pour into a glass filled with ice and garnish with the slice of lime and fresh mint.

watermelon, lime, and lemongrass juice

Serves 1

3 cups (456 g) peeled and cubed

   watermelon

$1/2$ teaspoon (1 g) grated fresh ginger

Ice cubes

2 tablespoons (30 ml) lime juice

2 tablespoons (30 ml) lemongrass

   syrup (page 6)

Run the melon and ginger through
a juice press. Pour the juice into a
glass filled with ice and add the
lime juice and lemongrass syrup.
Stir and serve. You can also make
this juice in a blender; it will be
thicker, but will taste just as good!

smoothies

A smoothie is a drink made with yogurt and ice cubes. You can add almost any kind of flavoring: fruits, berries, herbs, and sometimes spices. To make a smoothie, you will need a blender or a food processor that can crush ice. If you prefer, crush the ice cubes first and then add the ice to the smoothie after it is blended.

blueberry and vanilla smoothie

Serves 2

$2/3$ cup (100 g) blueberries, preferably frozen, plus extra
  blueberries, for garnish
$1/2$ large banana
$12/3$ cups (400 ml) plain yogurt
Seeds from $1/2$ vanilla bean
1 tablespoon (12.5 g) sugar, optional
6 ice cubes

Place all the ingredients except the garnish in a blender
and mix until smooth. Pour the smoothie into a glass and
garnish with the reserved blueberries.

melon, honey, and lime smoothie

Serves 2

2/3 cup (100 g) peeled, cubed honeydew melon
2 tablespoons (30 ml) honey
Juice of 1/2 lime
6 mint leaves, plus additional for garnish
1 1/4 cups (300 ml) plain yogurt
6 ice cubes
Lime slices, for garnish

Put the honeydew melon, honey, lime juice, 6 mint leaves, yogurt, and ice cubes into a blender and blend until smooth. Pour the smoothie into a glass and garnish with lime slices and reserved mint leaves.

coconut smoothie with ground nutmeg

Serves 2

1/2 lime
Grated coconut, for
    rimming glasses
1/2 cup (120 ml) milk
3/4 cup (180 ml)
    coconut milk
1/2 cup (120 ml)
    plain yogurt
1 large banana
6 ice cubes
Ground nutmeg, for
    garnish

Rub the lime around the rim of each glass and dip in the grated coconut to coat. You will get an attractive rim this way. Put the milk, coconut milk, yogurt, banana, and ice cubes in a blender and blend until smooth. Pour the smoothie into the two glasses and sprinkle a tiny bit of nutmeg on top of each.

strawberry smoothie

Serves 2

$3/4$ cup (200 g) strawberries, preferably frozen
1 large apricot, pitted and cubed
1 large banana
$1 2/3$ cups (400 ml) plain yogurt
6 ice cubes
$1/4$ cup (60 ml) strawberry sauce

Put the strawberries, apricot, banana, yogurt, and ice cubes in a blender and blend until smooth. Drizzle the strawberry sauce on the inside of two glasses, creating a striped pattern. Pour the smoothie gently into the glasses so you don't ruin the strawberry sauce stripes.

papaya smoothie

Serves 2

$3/4$ cup (100 g) cubed papaya, plus $1/3$ cup (50 g) for serving
1 tablespoon (15 ml) honey
$1 2/3$ cups (400 ml) plain yogurt
6 ice cubes

Put the $3/4$ cup (100 g) of papaya, honey, $1 1/4$ cups (300 ml) of the yogurt, and ice cubes into a blender and blend until smooth. Divide the rest of the yogurt between two glasses and carefully fill with the finished smoothie. Sprinkle some of the reserved papaya cubes over each glass and serve.

tropical smoothie

Serves 2

$2/3$ cup (100 g) cubed mango, plus additional for garnish

$2/3$ cup (100 g) pineapple chunks

1 large banana

$1 2/3$ cups (400 ml) plain yogurt

1 teaspoon (1.75 g) ground ginger

Juice of 1 lime

6 ice cubes

2 tablespoons (20 g) rolled oats, for garnish

Put the $2/3$ cup (100 g) of mango and the pineapple, banana, yogurt, ginger, lime juice, and ice cubes into a blender and blend until smooth. Pour the smoothie into a glass and garnish with the reserved mango and oats.

coffee, tea, and hot chocolate

Nothing is better to wake up to than the smell of freshly

brewed coffee. In our recipes we have used espresso, which

is more concentrated than regular coffee. You do not need to

run out and buy a huge, expensive espresso machine—the

simple, old-fashioned ones will produce the same results. The

only thing you need to make great coffee is fresh, clean water

and good coffee beans that are ground correctly. Coffee for

espresso must always be very finely ground.

You can make foamed milk with a milk steamer or a wand

mixer that you insert into the hot milk. If you do not have a

milk steamer or wand mixer, pour a little hot milk into a bottle

and shake well!

cappuccino

Serves 1

1 part brewed espresso

2 parts hot milk

1 part foamed milk (page 32)

Pinch of ground cinnamon,

  for garnish

Pour the espresso and hot milk into a tempered glass or cup, and top up with milk foam. Sprinkle a little ground cinnamon on top.

cortado

Serves 1

3 parts brewed
  espresso
1 part foamed milk
  (page 32)

Pour the espresso
into a small, tem-
pered glass or cup.
Add a little milk
foam on top and
serve.

hot chocolate with cinnamon

Serves 1

1.4 ounces (40 g) dark chocolate, preferably with a
high cocoa content
2 tablespoons (30 ml) water
3/4 cup (180 ml) milk
1 cinnamon stick
Pinch of ground cinnamon, for garnish

Put the chocolate and water into a small saucepan
and heat slowly over low heat. Stir the chocolate as
it melts. Add the milk and cinnamon stick. Bring the
hot chocolate to a boil and remove immediately
from the heat. Remove the cinnamon stick and
serve the hot chocolate with a pinch of ground
cinnamon on top.

café mocha

Serves 1

2 tablespoons (30 ml) chocolate syrup
2 parts brewed espresso
1 part hot milk
1 part foamed milk (page 32)
Pinch of grated chocolate, for garnish

Pour the chocolate syrup into a tempered glass or
cup. Add the espresso, hot milk, and foamed milk.
Garnish with grated chocolate.

con panna

Serves 1

2 parts brewed espresso

1 part partially whipped

  cream

Pour the espresso into a small, tempered glass or cup. Spoon the partially whipped cream gently on top and serve.

Serves 4

1²/₃ cups
  (400 ml)
  water
1 large cinnamon stick
8 cardamom seeds
2 slices of fresh ginger
3 teaspoons (6 g)
  Darjeeling tea
³/₄ cup (180 ml) hot milk
Sugar or honey
³/₄ cup (180 ml) foamed milk
  (page 32)
Pinch of ground cinnamon, for
  garnish

Bring the water, cinnamon stick, cardamom seeds, and ginger to a boil in a saucepan. Let simmer for about 10 minutes. Add the tea, remove from the heat, and set aside. Let the tea steep for about 5 minutes before straining it into a pitcher. Stir in the hot milk and sweeten to taste. Pour the tea into glasses, add a little milk foam on top, and finish with a little ground cinnamon.

chai lai tea

Serves 1

1 teaspoon (2 g) loose green tea

2 sprigs of fresh mint

1¼ cups (300 ml) boiling water

Honey

mint tea

Put the tea and mint into a heatproof pitcher and add the boiling water. Let the tea steep for 5 minutes before straining into a cup. Add honey to taste.

rosemary tea

Serves 1

1 teaspoon (2 g) loose breakfast tea

1 sprig fresh rosemary

1¼ cups (300 ml) boiling water

Honey

Put the tea and rosemary into a
heatproof pitcher and add the
boiling water. Let the tea steep for
5 minutes before straining into a cup.
Add honey to taste and serve.

Serves 1

1 teaspoon (2 g) loose

green tea

2 slices of fresh ginger

1¼ cups (300 ml) boiling

water

Honey

1 slice of lemon

ginger tea

Put the green tea and ginger into a heatproof pitcher and add the boiling water. Let the tea steep

for 5 minutes before straining into a cup. Add honey to taste and serve with a slice of lemon.

breakfast

baked plums with yogurt and almonds

Serves 4

10 plums

2 tablespoons (25 g) sugar

3/4 cup (180 ml) plain yogurt

2 tablespoons (20 g) slivered

  almonds

Preheat oven to 350°F (180°C). Cut the plums in half and remove the pits. Place the plums in an ovenproof baking pan and sprinkle with sugar. Bake the plums for about 7 minutes. Serve the warm plums with some of the syrup from the pan, yogurt, and slivered almonds.

Serves 4

4 bagels

1/2 cup (100 g) cream cheese

7 ounces (210 g) sliced smoked
  salmon

2 medium-size plum tomatoes,
  seeded and diced

1 scallion, finely chopped

1/4 red onion, finely chopped

1 tablespoon (3.75 g) chopped
  fresh dill or parsley

1 teaspoon (3.75 g) small capers

2 tablespoons (30 ml) lemon juice

1 tablespoon (15 ml) olive oil

bagels with smoked salmon and
tomato and caper salsa

Cut the bagels in half and spread with cream cheese. Spread the smoked salmon on the bottom halves
of the bagels. Stir together the tomatoes, scallion, red onion, dill, capers, lemon juice, and olive oil.
Layer the salsa over the salmon on the bagels, place the other bagel halves on top, and serve.

toast cups with eggs

Serves 4

4 slices of white bread
3 tablespoons (42 g) melted
 butter
4 eggs
Fresh arugula
Cherry tomatoes

Preheat the oven to 350°F (180°C). Cut the crusts off the bread and brush both sides of the slices with melted butter. Gently press each slice of bread into a six-cup muffin pan, to form four bread "cups." Half-fill the two empty cups with water. Break one egg into each bread cup. Bake the toast cups for about 5 minutes. Gently remove them from the pan and serve with freah arugula and cherry tomatoes.

breakfast muffins

You can make two types of muffins using this recipe: sweet with berries, or nuts and oats.

12 muffins

Batter base:

$1/2$ cup (100 g) butter

2 eggs

$2/3$ cup (130 g) sugar

1 cup (140 g) flour

1 teaspoon (5 g) baking powder

Nut muffins:

¼ cup (30 g) chopped walnuts

2 tablespoons (20 g) rolled oats

With berries:

⅓ cup (50 g) fresh or frozen berries

Preheat the oven to 425°F (225°C). Melt the butter in a small saucepan over low heat and then let it cool. In a medium-size bowl, stir the eggs and sugar together until the sugar has melted. Add the flour, baking powder, and melted butter. Stir well, but don't overbeat the batter.

For the nut muffins, add the walnuts and 1 tablespoon of the oats. Pour the batter into greased muffin pans. Don't fill more than two-thirds full, because the batter can overflow during baking. Sprinkle the remaining oats on top. Bake for 10 to 12 minutes and cool on a baking rack.

For the berry muffins, pour the batter into greased muffin pans. Don't fill more than two-thirds full, because the batter can overflow while baking. Press a few berries lightly into the top of the batter of each muffin. Bake for 10 to 12 minutes and cool on a baking rack.

zucchini and feta cheese omelet

Serves 4

2 tablespoons (30 ml) olive oil
2 scallions, finely chopped
1 medium-size zucchini, thinly sliced
2 tablespoons (7.5 g) chopped fresh parsley
Salt
Freshly ground black pepper
6 eggs
2 tablespoons (30 ml) water
$2/3$ cup (100 g) feta cheese

Preheat the oven to 350°F (180°C). Heat the olive oil in an oven-safe skillet, then lightly sauté the scallions and zucchini until soft. Add the parsley, salt, and pepper. In a separate bowl, stir the eggs and water together and then pour the mixture into the skillet. Sprinkle the feta cheese over the top and simmer for about 5 minutes over medium heat. Place the pan in the oven and let it bake for 5 minutes, until the eggs set and acquire a golden color. Serve with good farm bread and a little salad.

Serves 4

5 medium-size passion fruits
3 tablespoons (37.5 g) sugar
¼ cup (60 ml) water
2 tablespoons (28.5 g) butter
3 eggs
¼ cup (60 ml) milk
1 banana, sliced thinly
8 slices of white bread
Fresh raspberries

french toast with banana and passion fruit

Cut the passion fruits in half and scrape the pulp out into a saucepan. Add the sugar and water. Cook over medium heat until the mixture thickens. Remove from the heat and let cool slightly. Preheat a griddle lightly greased with butter over medium heat. In a bowl, beat together the eggs and milk. Make four banana sandwiches. Dip both sides of the sandwiches into the egg mixture and fry them on the preheated griddle, turning once, until golden on both sides. Cut the sandwiches into wedges and serve with warm passion fruit sauce and fresh raspberries.

yogurt with honey and berries

Serves 4

3 1/3 cups (780 ml) plain yogurt

2 cups (300 g) fresh berries, such as blueberries,

raspberries, or strawberries

3/4 cup (200 ml) liquid honey

Divide the yogurt and berries among four dessert glasses. Drizzle with honey and serve.

yogurt muesli with pears

Serves 4

1 1/3 cups (200 g) rolled oats

1 (15-ounce [425 g]) can of

   pears packed in light syrup

   or natural juices

3/4 cup (180 ml) plain yogurt

Put the oats in a medium-size bowl and pour 3/4 cup (180 ml) of the pear juice over them. Let the mixture sit for about 10 minutes before stirring in the yogurt. Divide the muesli among four bowls and serve with the pears.

moroccan pancakes

Super-simple
pancakes that
are fried only on
one side

Serves 4

3 cups (500 g) semolina or sifted
all-purpose flour
¼ cup (50 g) sugar
1 tablespoon (15 g) baking powder
2 cups (460 ml) warm water

To serve:
Plain yogurt
Fresh berries

In a medium-size bowl, stir together
the flour, sugar, baking powder, and
water. Let the batter sit for about 10
minutes. Heat a nonstick skillet over
medium heat. Pour a small amount
of batter onto the ungreased pan,
forming the shape of a little pan-
cake. Cook for 2 to 3 minutes with-
out turning, until golden brown.
They are done when the top is
entirely dry. Serve with yogurt and
fresh berries.

Serves 4

3 cups (456 g) cubed
   watermelon
2 tablespoons (7.5 g)
   chopped mint
1/4 cup (60 ml) lime juice
Lime wedges, for garnish

watermelon and mint salad

Put the watermelon, mint, and lime juice in a bowl and gently toss.
Divide the salad among four individual bowls and garnish with a lime
wedge.

daytime

lassishakecooLicedtea
emonade punch cockt.
sdaiquiricoffeesoupo
eletnoodlesnoonlass
nakecooLicedtealemo
adepunchcocktailsda
iiricoffeesoupomelet
odleslassishakecooL
edtealemonadepunch
ocktailsdaiquiricoffee

coolers

watermelon and chile cooler

Serves 1

1 1/3 cups (200 g) cubed watermelon

1 tablespoon (15 ml) chile syrup

  (page 6)

1 tablespoon (15 ml) lime juice

Crushed ice

Fresh mint, for garnish

Put the watermelon, chile syrup, and lime

juice into a blender and blend until smooth.

Pour the drink over crushed ice and garnish

with a sprig of mint.

blueberry and mint cooler

Serves 1

^{2}/3 cup (100 g) blueberries

Juice of ^{1}/2 lime

2 tablespoons (30 ml) cinnamon syrup (page 6)

3 fresh mint leaves, plus additional for garnish

1^1/2 cups (338 g) ice cubes

Put the blueberries, lime juice, cinnamon syrup, mint,

and ice cubes into a blender and blend until smooth.

Pour the drink into a glass and garnish with

fresh mint.

watermelon and ginger cooler

Serves 1

1 1/3 cups (200 g) cubed watermelon

Juice of 1/2 lemon

1 teaspoon (1.8 g) grated fresh ginger

1/2 cup (120 ml) soda water

1 1/2 cups (338 g) ice cubes

Put all the ingredients into a blender and blend until

smooth. Pour into a glass and serve.

shakes

strawberry shake

Put the strawberries, milk, vanilla ice cream, and vanilla sugar into a blender

and blend until smooth. Use red decorator's icing to make small dots on the

inside of a glass. Gently pour the shake into the glass and serve.

Serves 1

1⅓ cup (100 g) fresh or frozen

   strawberries

¾ cup (180 ml) milk

4 scoops of vanilla ice cream

½ teaspoon (2 g) vanilla sugar

Red decorator's icing, for garnish

mango and coconut shake

Serves 1

1½ cups (340 g) peeled and cubed mango

½ banana

¾ cup (180 ml) coconut milk

½ cup (120 ml) milk

2 tablespoons (30 ml) cardamom syrup (page 6)

6 ice cubes

Grated coconut

Put the mango, banana, coconut milk, milk, car-

damom syrup, and ice cubes in a blender and

blend until smooth. Pour the shake into a glass

and sprinkle a little grated coconut on top.

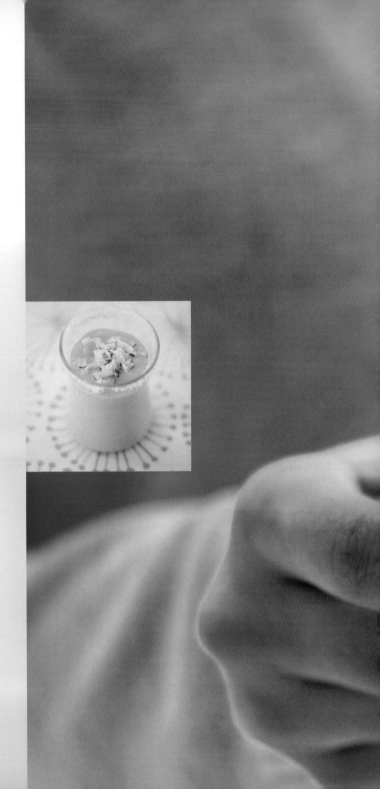

passion fruit shake with liqueur

Serves 1

2 large passion fruits

1 tablespoon (15 ml) Grand
   Marnier

3 scoops of vanilla ice cream

½ cup (100 ml) milk

Granulated sugar

Cut the passion fruits in half
and scrape their pulp into a
blender. Add the liqueur,
vanilla ice cream, and
milk. Blend until thick
and smooth. Add sugar
to taste, pour into a
glass, and serve.

Serves 1

½ cup (120 ml) brewed espresso, cooled
2 tablespoons (30 ml) chocolate syrup
3 scoops of vanilla ice cream
½ cup (120 ml) milk
2 tablespoons (30 ml) foamed milk (page 32)
Grated semisweet chocolate, for garnish

Put the espresso, chocolate syrup, vanilla ice cream, and milk into a blender and blend until thick and smooth. Pour the shake into a glass and spoon the milk foam on top. Garnish with some grated chocolate.

espresso shake

strawberry crush

Serves 1

½ cup (150 g) fresh or frozen strawberries, plus
   1 for garnish
1 tablespoon (15 ml) lemon juice
1 tablespoon (12.5 g) granulated sugar
½ cup (120 ml) soda water
8 ice cubes

Put the ½ cup of strawberries, lemon juice,
sugar, soda water, and ice cubes into a blender
and blend until thick and smooth. Pour the
drink into a glass and garnish with the
reserved strawberry.

crushes

lassi

banana and pear lassi

An Indian yogurt drink

Serves 1

1 banana
1 pear, cored and cut up
¾ cup (200 ml) plain yogurt
2 tablespoons (30 ml) cardamom syrup (page 6)
6 ice cubes
Pinch of ground cardamom, for garnish

Put the banana, pear, yogurt, cardamom syrup, and ice
cubes into a blender and mix until smooth. Pour the
lassi into a glass and top with a pinch of cardamom.

iced tea

Serves 1

8 raspberries

1¼ cups (300 ml) classic iced tea (see

opposite page)

Crushed ice

Crush the raspberries in the cold iced tea. Pour over crushed ice in a glass and serve.

raspberry iced tea

classic iced tea

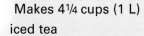

Makes 4¼ cups (1 L)
iced tea

1½ tablespoons (2 g)
loose Earl Grey tea
4¼ cups (1 L) boiling
water
¼ cup (50 g) sugar
1 slice of lemon
1 slice of lime
Ice cubes

Put the tea into a heat-proof pitcher and add the boiling water. Let the tea steep for 5 minutes before straining into another pitcher. Stir in the sugar and let the tea cool. Add the lemon and lime slices, and ice cubes and serve.

ginger and mint iced tea

Makes 4¼ cups (1 L) iced tea

1½ tablespoons (2 g) loose jasmine tea

4 slices of fresh ginger

1 lime, sliced

2 sprigs of fresh mint, plus additional for garnish

4¼ cups (1 L) boiling water

3 tablespoons (40 g) brown sugar

Ice cubes

Put the tea, ginger, lime, and mint into a heatproof pitcher. Add the boiling water and let the tea steep for 5 minutes. Strain the tea into another pitcher and add the sugar. Let the tea cool. Pour the tea into glasses filled with ice and garnish with fresh mint.

lemonade

lemonade

A concentrate that makes about 20 servings

6 organic lemons

4¼ cups (1 L) water

2¼ cups (450 g) sugar

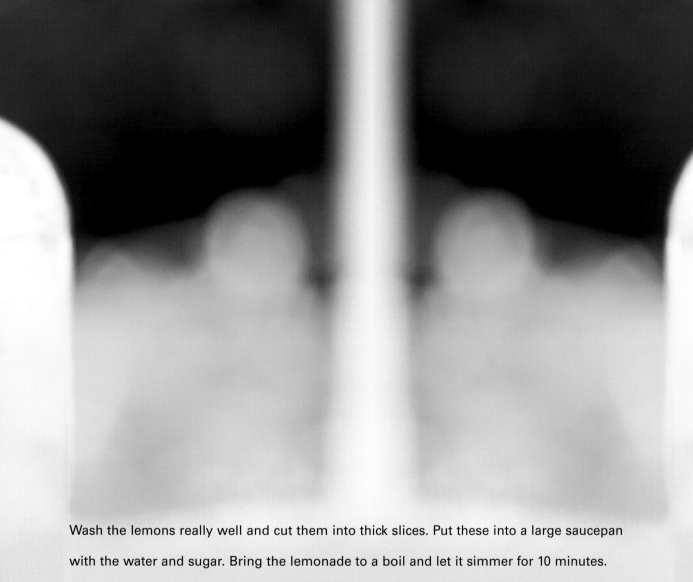

Wash the lemons really well and cut them into thick slices. Put these into a large saucepan with the water and sugar. Bring the lemonade to a boil and let it simmer for 10 minutes. Remove from the heat and let it cool. Keep the lemonade covered in the fridge for 24 hours before straining and storing in the fridge in a clean container. What you have now is a concentrate that needs to be mixed with water: 1 part lemonade to 3 parts water. Pour the diluted lemonade into a glass with lots of ice cubes and serve.

afternoon cocktails

bloody mary

Serves 1

1.5 ounces (45 ml) vodka
6.5 ounces (195 ml) tomato juice
A few drops of Worcestershire sauce
A few drops of Tabasco
1 tablespoon (15 ml) lemon juice
Ice cubes
1 celery stalk, for garnish
1 slice of lime, for garnish
Freshly ground pepper, for garnish

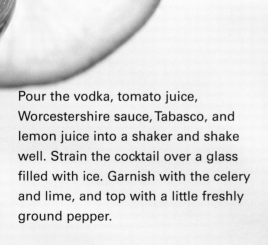

Pour the vodka, tomato juice,
Worcestershire sauce, Tabasco, and
lemon juice into a shaker and shake
well. Strain the cocktail over a glass
filled with ice. Garnish with the celery
and lime, and top with a little freshly
ground pepper.

long island
iced tea

Serves 1

Ice cubes
1 ounce (30 ml) vodka
1 ounce (30 ml) tequila
1 ounce (30 ml) Bacardi
0.5 ounce (15 ml) Cointreau
0.5 ounce (15 ml) lemon juice
0.5 ounce (15 ml) simple syrup
  (page 6)
1 ounce (30 ml) Coca-Cola
1 slice of lime, for garnish

Fill a highball glass with ice. Pour in the
ingredients, one after the other, and finish
with the Coca-Cola. If you pour really gently,
the Coke will settle on the bottom of the
glass. Garnish with a slice of lime and serve.

mimosa

Serves 1

0.3 ounce (9 ml) orange

  curaçao

1 ounce (30 ml) orange

  juice

Champagne

1 lemon stick (page 8)

Pour the curaçao and orange juice into a champagne glass. Top the rest of the glass with champagne

and garnish with the lemon stick.

pink lady

Serves 1

1 ounce (30 ml) light
   rum
1 tablespoon (12.5 g)
   sugar
Crushed ice
1 ounce (30 ml)
   cranberry juice
Soda water
Fresh raspberries, for
   garnish

Pour the rum and sugar into a glass filled with crushed ice and stir really well. Pour in the cranberry

juice and top up the rest of the glass with soda water. Garnish with raspberries and serve.

sangria

Makes about 33 ounces (1 L) or 6 servings

1 (750 ml) bottle Rioja red wine

3 tablespoons (37.5 g) sugar

1.5 ounces (45 ml) Cointreau

1.5 ounces (45 ml) lemon juice

Ice cubes

Lemon and lime slices

Fresh mint, for garnish

Pour the red wine, sugar, Cointreau, and lemon juice into a pitcher and stir really well. Add ice and the slices of lemon and lime. Garnish with mint and serve.

sparkling sangria

Makes about 33 ounces (1 L) or 6
 servings

1 orange, sliced

1 lime, sliced

6.5 ounces (195 ml) orange juice

6.5 ounces (195 ml) cranberry

 juice

16 ounces (480 ml) sparkling wine

Ice cubes

Fill a large pitcher with ice and add
all the ingredients. Stir gently and
serve chilled.

mint daze

Serves 1

1.25 ounces (40 ml) vodka

4 fresh mint leaves, sliced into

fine strips

0.75 ounce (20 ml) simple syrup

(page 6)

0.5 ounce (15 ml) lime juice

Crushed ice

Place the vodka, mint, simple syrup, and lime juice in a glass filled with crushed ice. Serve.

piña colada

Serves 1

1.5 ounces (45 ml) Bacardi
4 ounces (120 ml) pineapple juice
1 ounce (30 ml) coconut milk
0.5 ounce (15 ml) Malibu rum
0.5 ounce (15 ml) simple syrup (page 6)
1½ cups (338 g) ice cubes
1 slice of lime, for garnish

Place all the ingredients except the lime in a blender and blend until the mixture is smooth and the ice is totally crushed. Pour into a glass and garnish with the slice of lime.

strawberry daiquiri

Serves 1

8 large strawberries, plus 1 strawberry for garnish
1 ounce (30 ml) Bacardi
1 ounce (30 ml) Cointreau
1 ounce (30 ml) lemon juice
0.5 ounce (15 ml) simple syrup (page 6)
1½ cups (338 g) ice cubes

Place all the ingredients except the single strawberry in a blender and blend until the ice is completely crushed. Pour into a glass and garnish with the strawberry.

cranberry cocktail

Serves 1

Crushed ice

1 ounce (30 ml) vodka

1.25 ounces (40 ml) ginger ale

3.5 ounces (105 ml) cranberry juice

1 ice cube with berries (page 2)

Fill a glass with crushed ice; pour the

vodka, ginger ale, and cranberry juice

into the glass; and top with the berry

ice cube.

Serves 1

5 fresh mint leaves, plus additional

  for garnish

0.15 ounce (4 ml) simple syrup

  (page 6)

0.15 ounce (4 ml) water

Ice cubes

2 ounces (60 ml) bourbon

mint julep

Crush the five mint leaves in a glass with the simple syrup and water. Add the ice and bourbon. Stir well and garnish with fresh mint.

frozen daiquiri
with mango and papaya

Serves 1

2/3 cup (100 g) cubed mango or

papaya

1 ounce (30 ml) Bacardi

1 ounce (30 ml) Cointreau

0.5 ounce (15 ml) lemon juice

0.5 ounce (15 ml) simple syrup

(page 6)

1½ cups (338 g) ice cubes

Place all the ingredients in a blender and mix until all the ice is crushed. Pour the daiquiri into a glass and serve.

coffee

iced coffee mocha

Serves 1

2 tablespoons (30 ml) chocolate syrup
2 parts brewed espresso
1 part cold milk
Ice cubes
1 part foamed milk (page 32)
Grated semisweet chocolate, for garnish

Pour the chocolate syrup into a glass. Place
the espresso, milk, and ice in a shaker and
shake well. Strain the coffee into the glass.
Add the milk foam on top and garnish with
grated chocolate.

iced coffee latte

Serves 1

3 parts brewed espresso
1 tablespoon (14 g) brown sugar
Ice cubes
1 part foamed milk (page 32)

Place the espresso, brown sugar, and ice in
a shaker and shake well. Strain the coffee
into a glass and add the milk foam on top.

granita (frozen coffee)

Serves 1

7 ounces (210 ml) brewed espresso

1 tablespoon (14 g) brown sugar

1 teaspoon (5 ml) Amaretto

Put the espresso, sugar, and Amaretto into a frostproof bowl and stir until the sugar dissolves. Let the

coffee cool. Place the bowl in the freezer and stir every 30 minutes until the coffee is a grainy slush.

Serve in a glass.

coffee frappé

Serves 1

3 parts brewed espresso

1 tablespoon (15 ml) cinnamon syrup (page 6)

1 teaspoon (4 g) sugar

1 part heavy whipping cream

Ice cubes

Place all the ingredients in a shaker and shake well. Strain the coffee into a glass. Foam will be created from the shaking.

lunch

carrot and ginger soup

Serves 4

1/4 cup (60 ml) olive oil

6 large carrots, peeled and cut

   into cubes, plus grated

   carrot, for garnish

1-inch (2 cm) piece of fresh

   ginger, chopped

1 large potato, chopped

3 garlic cloves, minced

1 small onion, chopped

3 1/3 cups (780 ml) chicken stock

Salt

Freshly ground black pepper

Chopped fresh parsley, for

   garnish

Heat the olive oil in a large pan over medium heat. Sauté the cubed carrots, ginger, potato, garlic, and onion until the onions are soft. Transfer to a large stockpot, add the chicken stock, and let the soup simmer for 30 minutes. Pour the soup into a blender in several batches and blend until smooth; you can also use an immersion blender directly in the pot. Add salt and pepper to taste. Ladle into soup bowls and garnish with the parsley and grated carrot.

chicken and grapefruit salad with yogurt dressing

Serves 4

1 pound (454 g) skinless chicken breasts
Salt
Freshly ground black pepper
2 tablespoons (30 ml) olive oil
2 grapefruits, in sections
10 ounces (284 g) fresh arugula
10 cherry tomatoes, halved
2 tablespoons (15 g) pistachios
1¼ cups (300 ml) plain yogurt
2 tablespoons (30 ml) olive oil
1 tablespoon (15 ml) lemon juice
1 lime, wedged

Rub the chicken breasts with the salt and pepper and sauté in the olive oil over medium heat for about 3 minutes on each side. Let them rest for about 5 minutes before cutting into strips. Divide the chicken, grapefruit, arugula, tomatoes, and pistachios among four plates. In a separate bowl, stir together the yogurt, olive oil, and lemon juice. Add salt and pepper to taste. Pour the dressing over each salad and serve with the wedges of lime.

Serves 4

1 loaf of Italian bread, crust removed
6 tablespoons (90 ml) olive oil
1 garlic clove, chopped
1 head romaine lettuce, washed and dried

Dressing:
6 tablespoons (90 ml) olive oil
Pinch of salt
Freshly ground black pepper
1 tablespoon (15 ml) lemon juice
6 drops Worcestershire sauce
2 egg yolks
1/3 cup (30 g) grated Parmesan cheese

caesar salad

Preheat the oven to 400°F (200°C). Cut the crustless bread into long, thin strips. Put the bread strips in an ovenproof pan and brush with a mixture of the 6 tablespoons of oil and the garlic. Bake the bread for about 6 minutes or until brown. Shake the pan so the bread does not burn. Take the bread out of the oven and let cool. Divide the romaine lettuce and breadsticks among four glasses. Prepare the dressing: In a separate bowl, stir together the oil, salt, pepper, lemon juice, Worcestershire sauce, egg yolks, and Parmesan. Pour the dressing over the salad and serve.

Serves 4

2 large loaves of focaccia bread
½ cup (120 ml) prepared pesto
10 ounces (284 g) fresh arugula
8 slices of Parma or smoked
   ham
10–12 slices fresh mozzarella
   cheese
2 medium-size plum tomatoes,
   sliced
2 sprigs fresh basil

Slice the focaccia in half and
then in half again. Fill with the
pesto, arugula, Parma
ham, mozzarella,
tomatoes,
and basil
and
serve.

focaccia
with pesto, parma ham, and mozzarella

salmon and potato salad with lemon mayonnaise

Serves 4

Lemon mayonnaise:
1 egg yolk
Zest of 1 lemon, grated finely
3 tablespoons (45 ml) lemon juice
1–1 ¼ cups (240 ml) soybean oil
Salt
Freshly ground black pepper

14 ounces (400 g) salmon fillets
Olive oil
12 small potatoes, boiled and cut in half
10 ounces (284 g) fresh arugula
2 tablespoons (6.5 g) fresh dill
1 lemon, cut into wedges

Make the mayonnaise: Mix the egg yolk, lemon zest, and lemon juice in a bowl. Slowly pour in the oil in a thin stream while whisking. Continue until you have added all the oil and you have a thick and smooth mayonnaise. If it separates, just add a little cold water and continue beating. Add salt and pepper to taste.

Rub the salmon with salt and pepper, and sauté in the olive oil over medium heat for about 2 minutes on each side. Let the salmon cool and cut it into pieces. Arrange the salmon, potatoes, arugula, and dill on the plates. Divide the mayonnaise and serve each portion with a lemon wedge.

pepper omelet with parma ham
and mozzarella

Serves 4

2 tablespoons (30 g) butter

6 eggs

6 tablespoons (90 ml) water

Salt

1 teaspoon (2 g) freshly

ground pepper

10 ounces (248 g) fresh

arugula

10–12 slices fresh mozzarella

cheese

6 slices Parma ham

10 cherry tomatoes, halved

6 tablespoons (90 ml) olive

oil

1 teaspoon (5 ml) balsamic

vinegar

Melt the butter over low heat in a skillet. In a bowl, beat the eggs, water, salt, and pepper together. Pour the egg mixture into the pan. Cook the omelet, covered, over medium heat for about 5 minutes; turn it and cook for another 3 minutes on the other side. Put the omelet on a plate and arrange with arugula, mozzarella, Parma ham, and cherry tomatoes. In a small bowl, stir together the olive oil and balsamic vinegar, and pour over the omelet. Grind lots of black pepper over it and serve with bread.

pasta salad with tuna

Serves 4

14 ounces (400 g) penne

  pasta

Salt

14 ounces (400 g) fresh tuna

Freshly ground black pepper

1 tablespoon (15 ml) olive oil

10 ounces (284 g) fresh

  spinach, rinsed

1 pound (454 g) sugar snap

  peas

12 cherry tomatoes, halved

Dressing:

6 tablespoons (90 ml) olive oil

1 teaspoon (5 ml) balsamic

  vinegar

1 tablespoon (15 ml) lemon

  juice

Zest of ½ lemon, grated finely

Salt and pepper

Cook the pasta in salted water until al dente. Drain and let the pasta cool under cold, running water. Rub the tuna with salt and pepper. Sear the tuna in olive oil over high heat, about 30 seconds on each side. Remove from the heat and cut it into chunks. Mix the pasta, tuna, spinach, sugar snap peas, and tomatoes in a bowl. In a separate bowl, mix together the ingredients for the dressing and add salt and pepper to taste. Pour the dressing over the salad and serve.

evening

cosmopolitantrozenc
moflirtinipunchmoji
caipirinhacubalibrepa
iontinipunchcasabla
anightkirroyalebelli
margaritacosmopolit
frozencosmoflirtini
chmojitocaipirinhac
alibrepassiontinipur
asablanenightkirro

classic drinks

seabreeze

Serves 1

Crushed ice

1 ounce (30 ml) vodka

1.5 ounces (45 ml) grapefruit juice

0.75 ounce (20 ml) cranberry juice

Fill a glass with crushed ice. Pour in the vodka and grapefruit juice, and finish by floating the cranberry juice gently on top.

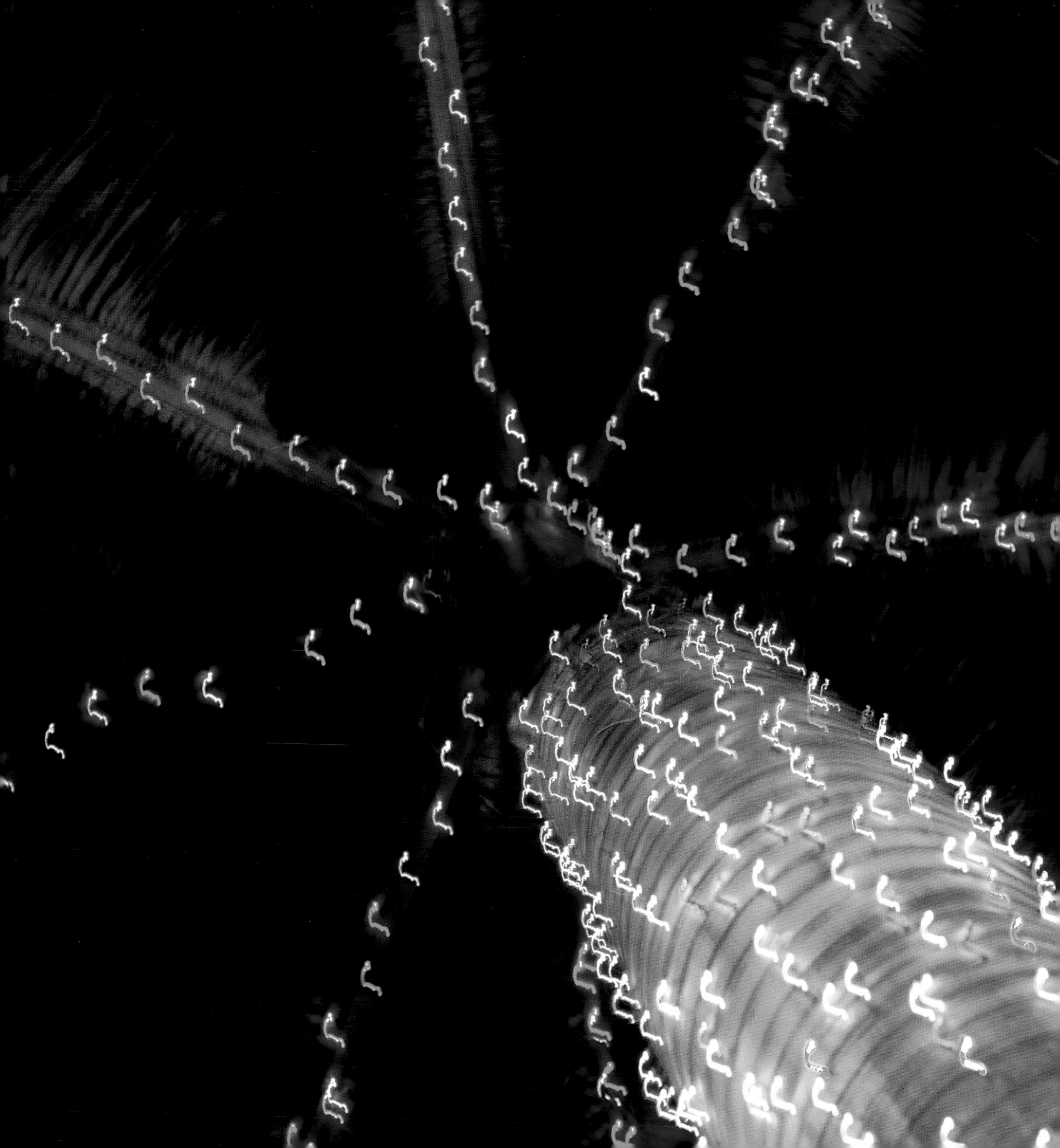

mai thai

Serves 1

1.75 ounces (50 ml) rum

0.5 ounce (15 ml) orange curaçao

0.5 ounce (15 ml) apricot brandy

0.5 ounce (15 ml) lime juice

Dash of Angostura bitters

Dash of simple syrup (page 6)

0.5 ounce (15 ml) pineapple juice

Ice cubes

Fresh mint, for garnish

Place all the ingredients except the mint in a shaker and shake well. Strain into a glass and garnish with mint.

margarita

Serves 1

1 slice of lime

Coarse salt

1.75 ounces (50 ml) tequila

0.75 ounce (20 ml) Cointreau

Juice of $\frac{1}{2}$ lime

Crushed ice

Run the slice of lime around the edge of the glass and then dip it in coarse salt to coat the rim. Pour all the remaining ingredients into a shaker and shake well. Strain into the prepared glass and serve.

blue margarita

Serves 1

1 ounce (30 ml) tequila

0.25 ounce (7 ml) Triple Sec

1 tablespoon (15 ml) lime juice

0.25 ounce (7 ml) blue curaçao

1½ teaspoons (6.25 g) sugar

Ice cubes

1 slice of lemon

Place the tequila, Triple Sec, lime juice, curaçao, sugar, and ice in a shaker. Shake well. Pour the margarita into a glass and serve with a slice of lemon.

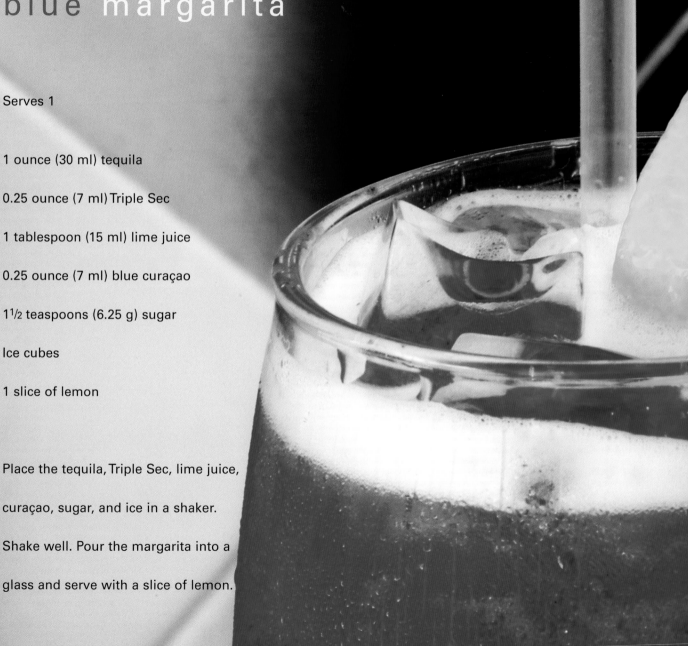

white russian

Serves 1

Ice cubes

1 ounce (30 ml) Kahlúa

1 ounce (30 ml) vodka

1 ounce (30 ml) heavy

whipping cream

Fill a glass with ice. Pour in the remaining ingredients and stir well. Serve.

bellini

Serves 1

$1/2$ peach, pitted

Chilled champagne

Run the peach through a blender until it is completely pureed. Pour into a glass and top off with champagne. Serve.

kir

Serves 1

0.5 ounce (15 ml) crème de cassis

Chilled, dry white wine

Pour the crème de cassis into a
tall glass and top off with white
wine. Serve.

kir royale

Serves 1

0.5 ounce (15 ml) crème de cassis

Chilled champagne

Pour the crème de cassis into a
champagne flute and top off with
champagne. Serve.

mojito

Serves 1

3 fresh mint sprigs
2 tablespoons (30 ml) simple syrup (page 6)
2 tablespoons (30 ml) lime juice
Crushed ice
1.75 ounces (50 ml) dark rum
Soda water

Pour the mint, simple syrup, and lime juice into a glass. Use the back of a spoon to muddle the mint in the glass. Add crushed ice and the rum, and top off with soda water.

nuts with coriander and sugar

Serves 8

5.25 ounces (150 g) hazelnuts
5.25 ounces (150 g) almonds
3.5 ounces (100 g) pecans
2 tablespoons (25 g) sugar
1 tablespoon (18 g) coarse salt
1 teaspoon (0.5 g) ground coriander
$1/2$ teaspoon (1 g) cayenne

Preheat the oven to 350°F (180°C). Spread all the nuts on a baking sheet. Sprinkle with the sugar, salt, coriander, and cayenne. Bake for 4 minutes. Stir and let the nuts bake for another 5 minutes. Remove from the oven and let cool. Enjoy.

caipirinha

Serves 1

$1/2$ lime, cut into wedges, plus additional
   for garnish
1 teaspoon (4 g) sugar
1.75 ounces (50 ml) cachaca
Crushed ice

Put the half-lime worth of wedges and the sugar into a glass and crush the lime with the back of a spoon. Pour in the cachaca and stir well. Top off with crushed ice and garnish with lime wedges.

peach cobbler

Serves 1

2 thin slices of peach

Chilled champagne

Put the peach slices in a tall champagne flute and top off with chilled champagne. Serve.

blue heaven

Serves 1

1 ounce (30 ml) rum

0.5 ounce (15 ml) Amaretto

0.5 ounce (15 ml) blue

curaçao

0.5 ounce (15 ml) lime juice

2.5 ounces (75 ml) pineapple

juice

Ice cubes

1 lime wedge, for garnish

Place all the ingredients except the lime wedge in a shaker and shake well. Pour into a glass and garnish with the lime wedge.

cosmopolitan

Serves 1

0.3 ounce (9 ml) lemon vodka
0.5 ounce (15 ml) vodka
0.75 ounce (20 ml) Cointreau
2 ounces (60 ml) cranberry juice
Ice cubes

Place all the ingredients in a shaker and shake well. Strain into a martini glass and serve.

sweet potato chips

Serves 8

6 large sweet potatoes
1 2/3 cups (400 ml) corn oil
Coarse salt

Cut the potatoes into thin slices, using a sharp knife or mandoline. Heat the oil in a deep skillet; it is hot enough when it bubbles around a wooden skewer. Fry a small amount of the sweet potato slices at a time for about 6 minutes or until golden brown. Remove with a slotted spoon and drain on paper towels. Sprinkle with coarse salt and serve.

singapore sling

Serves 1

Dash of Angostura bitters
1 ounce (30 ml) gin
0.5 ounce (15 ml) Triple Sec
0.5 ounce (15 ml) grenadine
0.5 ounce (15 ml) cherry liqueur
0.5 ounce (15 ml) lime juice
1 ounce (30 ml) pineapple juice
1 ounce (30 ml) orange juice
Ice cubes
1 slice of lime, for garnish

Place all the ingredients except the lime in a
shaker and shake well. Strain into a tall glass and
garnish with the slice of lime.

gin fizz

Serves 1

1.75 ounces (50 ml) gin

1 tablespoon (15 ml)

  lemon juice

1 teaspoon (4 g) sugar

¼ teaspoon (1.25 ml)

  egg white

Ice cubes

Soda water

Place the gin, lemon juice, sugar, egg white, and ice cubes in

a shaker and shake well. Strain into a glass and top off with

soda water.

casablanca

Serves 1

1 ounce (30 ml) rum

3 ounces (90 ml) pineapple

juice

1 ounce (30 ml) coconut milk

0.25 ounce (7 ml) grenadine

Ice cubes

1 slice of lime, for garnish

1 slice of pineapple, for

garnish

Place all the ingredients except the lime and pineapple slices in a shaker and shake well. Pour into a tall

glass and garnish with the slices of lime and pineapple.

modern drinks

cointreau sunset

Serves 1

Crushed ice

1 ounce (30 ml) Cointreau

0.35 ounce (10 ml) grenadine

3.5 ounces (105 ml) orange

juice

Fill a glass with crushed ice.
Pour in the Cointreau and
grenadine. Carefully float the
orange juice along the edges
so it layers.

captain nemo

Serves 1

1.75 ounces (50 ml)

Cointreau

0.75 ounce (20 ml) blue

curaçao

1 ounce (30 ml) sweet-

and-sour mix

Dash of orange juice

Ice cubes

ce all the ingredients in a shaker and shake well. Strain the drink into a glass
h a prepared sugared rim (see page 10) and serve.

citron crush

Serves 1

1 ounce (30 ml) lemon vodka

0.75 ounce (20 ml) simple syrup

  (page 6)

1 tablespoon (15 ml) lemon juice

Crushed ice

Grated lemon zest, for garnish

Pour the vodka, simple syrup, and lemon juice into a shaker and

shake well. Fill a glass with crushed ice and pour in the cocktail.

Sprinkle a little grated lemon zest over the top and serve.

peach passion

Serves 1

Ice cubes

1 ounce (30 ml) peach juice

1 ounce (30 ml) gin

2 ounces (60 ml) ginger ale

Put the ice in a highball glass

and pour in the rest of the

ingredients. Stir gently and

serve.

Serves 1

1 plum, pitted and

  pureed

Ice cubes

1 teaspoon (4 g) sugar

1 ounce (30 ml) vodka

Soda water

plush plum

Put the plum puree, ice cubes, sugar, and vodka in a shaker. Shake well. Pour the drink into a glass and

top off with soda water.

raspberry rush

Serves 1

1/4 cup (50 g)
    raspberries
1 tablespoon
    (15 ml) lemon
    juice
1 tablespoon
    (12.5 g) sugar
0.35 ounce (10
    ml) rum
0.35 ounce (10
    ml) Cointreau
Ice cubes
Soda water

Put the raspberries, lemon juice, sugar, Bacardi, Cointreau, and
ice in a blender and blend. Pour the drink into a glass and top off
with soda water. Stir and enjoy!

Serves 1

Crushed ice

0.5 ounce (15 ml) light rum

0.5 ounce (15 ml) Triple Sec

0.5 ounce (15 ml) Midori

1 tablespoon (15 ml) lemon

juice

0.5 ounce (15 ml) blue curaçao

opal ice

Fill a glass with ice. Pour the rum, Triple Sec, Midori, and lemon juice

into a shaker with a little ice and shake. Pour the cocktail into the

glass and float the blue curaçao on top.

Five drinks that all girls love and all boys need to know how to make

1. Cosmopolitan

2. Martinis, all of them

3. Margarita

4. Kir Royale

5. Bellini

Five drinks that all boys love and all girls need to know how to make

1. Rusty Nail

2. White Russian

3. Bloody Mary

4. Mint Julep

5. Dry martini (let him believe he is James Bond)

sorbet-vodka shot

Serves 1

1 scoop of strawberry sorbet

1 ounce (30 ml) vodka

Put the sorbet in a glass and pour the vodka over it. Can be eaten using a little spoon.

moscow mule

Serves 1

Crushed ice

1.75 ounces (50 ml)

 vodka

1 lime wedge

Ginger ale

Fill up a glass with crushed ice. Pour in the vodka and crush the lime wedge in the glass, using the back

of a spoon. Top off with ginger ale and serve with a straw.

Serves 1

3 strawberries

6 blackberries

1 ounce (30 ml) simple syrup

 (page 6)

1 ounce (30 ml) vodka

Ice cubes

berry vodka ice

Put all the ingredients into a blender and blend until

the ice is crushed. Pour the drink into a glass and

serve.

passiontini

Serves 1

1 ounce (30 ml) vodka
0.75 ounce (20 ml) passion fruit liqueur
0.35 ounce (10 ml) cranberry juice
Dash of lime juice
Ice cubes
Crushed ice

Place the vodka, passion fruit liqueur, cranberry juice, lime juice, and ice cubes in a shaker and shake well. Strain the cocktail into a martini glass filled with crushed ice and serve.

flirtini

Serves 1

1 ounce (30 ml) vodka
0.35 ounce (10 ml) apricot liqueur
0.35 ounce (10 ml) cranberry juice
0.35 ounce (10 ml) pineapple juice
Ice cubes
Champagne
1 strawberry, for garnish

Place the vodka, apricot liqueur, cranberry juice, pineapple juice, and ice cubes in a shaker and shake well. Strain the cocktail into a martini glass and top off with champagne. Garnish with the strawberry.

all in one bowl

tropical punch

Serves 10

Ice cubes
1 mango
1 papaya
10 strawberries
1 cup (240 ml) apple juice
1 cinnamon stick
3 cups (700 ml) ginger ale
1 bottle (750 ml) champagne
Fresh mint leaves

Fill a large bowl with ice cubes. Peel the mango and papaya, seed them, and cut their pulp into tiny cubes. Slice the strawberries in half. Fill the bowl with the fruit, apple juice, cinnamon stick, and ginger ale, and top off with the champagne. Garnish with mint.

ginger punch

Serves 10

1 bottle (750 ml) sparkling white wine
4 cups (1 L) ginger ale
2 cups (500 ml) pineapple juice
Juice of 1 lemon
Ice cubes
Fresh berries of your choice

Pour the sparkling white wine, ginger ale, pineapple juice, and lemon juice into a pitcher. Stir well and add the ice cubes and fresh berries.

Serves 8

10 ounces (300 g) assorted olives

1 red chile pepper, chopped finely

2 garlic cloves, chopped finely

6 tablespoons (90 ml) olive oil

1 tablespoon (8.5 g) capers

1 tablespoon (3 g) chopped fresh chives

Mix all the ingredients in a bowl. Marinate overnight before you serve with a great-tasting drink or a glass of beer.

kick-ass olives

tuna slices

Serves 8

7 ounces (200 g) fresh tuna
Salt
Freshly ground black pepper
2 tablespoons (30 ml) olive oil
1 cucumber, sliced
1 red chile pepper, chopped finely
2 tablespoons (19 g) chopped
   peanuts
1 tablespoon (3 g) chopped fresh
   chives

Rub the tuna with salt and pepper.
Heat the oil in a skillet over high
heat. Sear the tuna for 30 seconds
on each side. Remove from the
heat, cool, and cut into eight slices.
Divide the cucumber slices among
eight plates and place a tuna slice
on top of each cucumber slice.
Distribute the red chile, peanuts,
and chives over the top and serve.

mini pies with goat cheese and rosemary

Serves 8

1 (8-ounce) (227 g) package phyllo dough

5 ounces (150 g) goat cheese

1 cup (240 ml) heavy whipping cream

1 egg

2 egg yolks

Pinch of pepper

Fresh rosemary sprigs

Preheat the oven to 400°F (200°C). Keeping the unused dough beneath a damp paper towel while you work, quickly divide the phyllo dough into small sheets. Press the sheets into eight cups of a twelve-cup muffin pan so they form small piecrusts. In a bowl, stir together the goat cheese, cream, egg, egg yolks, and pepper. Fill the piecrusts with the goat cheese mixture, stick a rosemary sprig in each, fill the four empty cups partway with water, and bake the pies for 6 to 8 minutes. Serve warm.

Serves 8

2 tablespoons (25 g) active dry yeast

2 cups (460 ml) lukewarm water

3½ cups (490 g) all-purpose flour

6 tablespoons (90 ml) olive oil

1 teaspoon (6 g) salt

20 cherry tomatoes, halved

Fresh rosemary

Coarse salt

Olive oil

Dissolve the yeast in the water. Add the flour, olive oil, and salt. Knead the dough. Set in a greased bowl and let it rise in a warm place for 1 hour. Preheat the oven to 400°F (200°C). Divide the dough into twenty-four pieces and shape into small, round pizzas approximately 3 inches (8 cm) in diameter, ½ inch (1 cm) thick. Place them on a greased baking sheet. Layer the tomatoes on top and sprinkle with a few small pieces of rosemary, the salt, and a little olive oil. Bake for 6 to 8 minutes. Serve warm.

mini focaccia with tomatoes and rosemary

shrimp with coriander and lime

Serves 8

16 medium shrimp
16 skewers, soaked in water for 30 minutes
Juice of 1 lime, plus additional for serving
2 teaspoons (10 ml) Asian fish sauce
2 tablespoons (2 g) chopped fresh coriander
1 teaspoon (2 g) grated fresh ginger

Wash the shrimp, shell, and devein, leaving the tails intact.
Thread one shrimp lengthwise on each skewer. Put on a plate
and sprinkle with lime juice, fish sauce, coriander, and ginger. Let
the shrimp marinate in the refrigerator for at least 1 hour and
then grill for 30 seconds on each side. Squeeze a little lime juice
over them and serve warm.

spring rolls with crab and chile

Serves 8

7 ounces (200 g) crabmeat
1 red chile, finely chopped
1 tablespoon (15 ml) Asian fish sauce
1 carrot, grated
1/2 cup (50 g) bean sprouts
1 (8-ounce) (227 g) package phyllo sheets
1 egg yolk, beaten
1 1/4 cups (300 ml) corn oil
Sweet chile sauce, for serving

In a bowl, mix the crabmeat, chile, fish sauce, carrot, and bean sprouts together. Keeping the unused dough beneath a damp paper towel while you work, quickly cut the phyllo sheets into 4-inch (10 cm) squares. Put a little of the mixture in each sheet and roll tightly. Glue the edges with the beaten egg yolk. Heat the oil in a skillet; it is hot when it bubbles around a wooden skewer. Fry the spring rolls until golden brown, turning once. Serve warm, with sweet chile sauce.

gazpacho with shrimp

Serves 8

½ seedless cucumber
1 red bell pepper
1 jalapeño
1 small red onion
2 tablespoons (2 g) chopped cilantro
1 cup (240 ml) tomato juice
2 tablespoons (30 ml) olive oil
2 tablespoons (30 ml) lime juice
Salt
Freshly ground black pepper
8 marinated shrimp (page 150)

Chop all the vegetables and place them in a food processor with the cilantro, tomato juice, olive oil, and lime juice. Process until smooth. Add salt and pepper to taste. Chill the soup and pour into glasses. Serve with a marinated skewered shrimp on each glass.

nightcaps

rusty nail

Serves 1

Ice cubes

1.5 ounces (45 ml) whiskey

0.75 ounce (20 ml) Drambuie

Fill a glass with ice and pour in the whiskey and Drambuie. Stir slightly and serve.

hot toddy

Serves 1

2 ounces (60 ml)

  whiskey

1 teaspoon (5 ml)

  honey

1 cinnamon stick

1 slice of lemon

Boiling water

Pour the whiskey into a tempered glass or mug. Add the honey, cinnamon stick, and slice of lemon, and

top off with boiling water. Stir with the cinnamon stick and serve.

hot eggnog

Serves 1

0.5 ounce (15 ml) dark rum

0.5 ounce (15 ml) brandy

0.25 ounce (7 ml) simple syrup

  (page 6)

1 egg

Hot milk

Pinch of ground cinnamon,

  for garnish

Put the rum, brandy, simple syrup, and egg into a blender and process until completely blended. Pour

the mixture into a glass and top off with hot milk. Sprinkle a little cinnamon on top and serve.

glühwein
(mulled wine)

Serves 1

10 ounces (300 ml) red
wine

1 teaspoon (4 g) brown
sugar

1 cinnamon stick

1 slice of lemon

1 slice of orange

Put all the ingredients in a saucepan and heat slowly. Do not let the wine come to a boil. Pour the hot wine into a tempered glass, stir with the cinnamon stick, and serve.

amaretto coffee

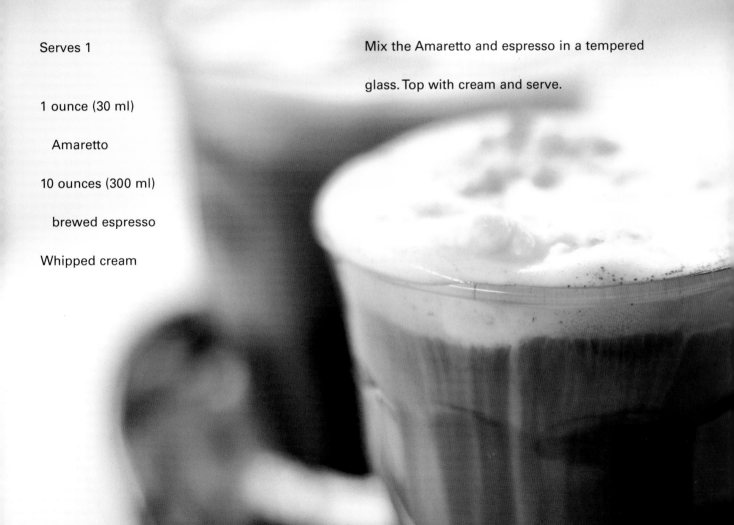

Serves 1

1 ounce (30 ml)

Amaretto

10 ounces (300 ml)

brewed espresso

Whipped cream

Mix the Amaretto and espresso in a tempered

glass. Top with cream and serve.

the day after

Ten great tips for surviving the day after

1. Water-water-water.

2. Stay in bed (call in sick to work).

3. Sweat it out. Sex or sauna!

4. Rose oil on the forehead.

5. Eat some salt.

6. Eat something sweet.

7. Take loads of vitamin C.

8. Get a massage (can lead to sex).

9. Eat dry toast.

10. Continue drinking!

a glass of water and an alka-seltzer

Need we say more?

orange juice with lemon
lots of vitamin c!

Serves 1

Juice of 2 oranges

Juice of ¼ lemon

Sugar

Pour the juices into a glass and add

sugar to taste. Stir well and enjoy.

eggs and bacon

We highly doubt you need a recipe for this perfect "the day after" breakfast.

tomatoes with olive oil

Sun-ripened tomatoes are a great medicine for the day after. You will double the effect if you pour some extra-virgin olive oil over them.

croque monsieur

Serves 4

1³/₄ cups (200 g) grated
   Cheddar cheese
1 tablespoon (16 g) Dijon
   mustard
1 egg yolk
8 slices of white bread
4 slices of ham
Cherry tomatoes, marinated
   in olive oil

Preheat the oven to 400°F (200°C). Mix the cheese, mustard, and egg yolk in a bowl. Place four slices of bread on a baking sheet. Layer the ham on top of the bread and put another slice of bread on top of each. Divide the cheese mixture and spread on top. Bake for 8 minutes. Serve with some cherry tomatoes marinated in olive oil.

tomato juice with tabasco

Serves 1

3/4 cup (180 ml)

tomato juice

3 drops of Tabasco

Pour the juice into a

glass and add the

Tabasco—enjoy!

index